MW01025504

THE
HISTORY OF
JESUS'
BIRTH, DEATH

AND WHAT IT MEANS
TO YOU AND ME

BY

ELIJAH MUHAMMAD

MESSENGER OF ALLAH

A
SECRETARIUS MEMPS PUBLICATION

THE HISTORY OF JESUS' BIRTH, DEATH AND WHAT IT MEANS TO YOU AND ME

Copyright 1993, by
M.E.M.P.S. PUBLICATIONS CO.

First Edition Released 1994
Second Printing 1995
Third Printing 1997

Published by
**MESSENGER ELIJAH MUHAMMAD
PROPAGATION SOCIETY
(M.E.M.P.S.)**

P.O. BOX 162412 • ATLANTA, GA 30321

All Rights Reserved. No part of this book may be reproduced or transmitted in any form by any means, electronic, photocoping, mechanical, recording, information storage or retrieval system without permission from the publisher - MEMPS - Brief quotations may be used in reviews or commentary.

**FOR 24HR
RETAIL CATALOG & WHOLESALE INFORMATION
770 907-2212**

ISBN # 1-884855-07-5

*Dedicated To Those
Who Will Stand For Truth
Even If It Is Against
Themselves.*

Table of Content

Acknowledgement

We seek the assistance of Allah (God), Who came in the Person of Master Fard Muhammad, through His Last and Greatest Messenger, the Most Honorable Elijah Muhammad.

We can never thank them enough for the Supreme Wisdom which has been showered upon us, and as the Messenger himself stated, "He (Allah) gave it to me like a flowing spring or flowing fountain. The fountain has enough drink in it to give everyone drink who comes to drink. YOU DON'T NEED A NEW FOUNTAIN, JUST TRY AND DRINK UP WHAT THIS FOUNTAIN HAS." Therefore, we avail ourselves of that water without hesitation, because we never get full. This means that the need for another fountain is totally obsolete.

I would like to thank the Hakim family, Rose, Dur're, Taqqee, Junaid and Khalfani, also Brother Azzam Waathiq Basit for their hard work contributed to make this work of the Messenger accessible to our people. May Allah, Master Fard Muhammad, continue to bless our continued effort and labor.

As-Salaam-Alaikum

Nasir M. Hakim, Founder
SECRETARIUS MEMPS

FOREWORD

While compiling these rare articles of Messenger Elijah Muhammad, and following the progression of how the Messenger presented such supreme wisdom, it opened up so many avenues of understanding until it makes one feel that beforehand they themselves knew nothing at all. What comes to mind is the old adage: The more you learn the more you come to know that you don't know anything.

This is a rewarding feeling because it serves to meter one's level of humility and capacity to learn more. For as many of us can see, we read different writings of the Honorable Elijah Muhammad, Last and Greatest Messenger of Allah, and although it affects us all differently, one thing is for sure, it will affect you. How one deals with the effect is very important, because after reading this profound history of Jesus, as only Allah's Last Messenger can explain with unparalleled depth, then the reader will see that even though Jesus had the truth and made an excellent attempt at acting on that truth, further study by him had revealed that he was not the one he thought he was, and that, that one, was yet to come 2,000 years later.

This aspect is so very, very profound. I say this because today, now that the Honorable Elijah Muhammad is no longer among us, many are coming forth and acting out what affect the truth is having on them. Many have actually ate dinner with the Messenger. Others were taught and trained by Him; some have had personal audiences with Him; some, although they were part of the Nation of Islam for years, would only see the Messenger once a year at the Annual Saviour's Day Convention held in Chicago, every February 26; while others were only babies or teen age prior to 1975, and have never met nor personally seen the Messenger. What would such personal contact mean if, one never internalizes what he or she had been taught for over 40 years?

Have you not learned that word is bond and bond is life and that you will lose your life if your word fails. Our brother Jesus did a great work, but as the Messenger said, had he not given up his life, we wouldn't even be talking about him today. He gets an honorable mention because he realized that he was in another man's place and what he was preaching was too soon; therefore, he, himself, had to pay. He accepted the hard fact and graciously got out of the way of the eventuality of prophesy to take its course. For him submitting to the truth, even though it meant giving up his life in the process, he demonstrated what he preached. This was the best of the few choices he could take.

We today must learn from this history, for how can we call ourselves ministers of the Greatest Messenger that ever lived with nothing significant to show. We must stop masquerading around here in our IGNORANCE saying we represent an All Wise God and His Greatest Messenger! We may find ourselves making mockery of what we believe in.

This helps the wise and humble among us to see that although we may mean well, if we are taking these titles and are not qualified by what the Messenger prescribes, and are justified by your works, you then may be contributing to confusing our people even further; consequently, developing one's self into an enemy of Allah rather than a helper. Take it or let it alone.

ARTICLE NO. 1 JULY 20, 1957

THE HISTORY OF JESUS
ISLAM, THE TRUE RELIGION,
THE SO-CALLED NEGROES' SALVATION

*The History of Jesus' Birth, Death
and What It Means to You and Me*

I won't be able to give a complete knowledge in one article. It will take a series of articles to tell of all the Prophets of God who are recorded in the Bible and Holy Qur'an Sharrieff. None is more controversial than the history of Jesus and none is more misunderstood. This misunderstanding is nearly 100 per cent among the so-called Negroes in the U.S.A., due to their following and believing what their enemies (the devils) have taught and written concerning Jesus' birth and death.

I do believe that if my poor blind, deaf and dumb people could be taught the truth of the true history of Jesus, they would awaken at once. Some of the so-called Negroes' leaders (preachers) are dumber to what the knowledge of Jesus' birth, life and death means than those who are following him, and for the sake of being called a leader (preacher) they are proud against the truth, and they will oppose it fearing the losses of their office. Thus-leading themselves and their followers to hell with the devils because of their blindness, love and fear of the devils.

I will teach you the truth as I have received it from Him-who is the Author of Truth-regardless to whom or what, for I speak not of myself-for I, too, was once blind, deaf and dumb, but I speak and write that which I have received of Him (Allah), and on Him do I rely.

2

There is no mentioning of Jesus in the history of Moses (Deut. 18:15-18). This cannot refer to the Jesus of 2,000 years ago, nor (Isaiah 9:6), nor even the 53rd chapter of Isaiah. For you disbelievers and blind guides who want me to prove what I teach, take a look at his history as recorded in the Holy Qur'an Sharrieff (3:41, 42, 44, 46), and try comparing it with the Bible's birth of Jesus.

When the angels said: "O mary, surely Allah gives you good news with a word from Him (of one) whose name is the Messiah, Jesus, Son of Mary, worthy of regards in this world and the hereafter."

NOTE: In the verse above, Jesus is called according to Arabic transliteration "Al-Masih, Isa and Ibn-i-Maryan," meaning in English, the Messiah, Son of Mary. "Masih," says the commentator on the language, means either one who travels much or one wiped over with some such thing as oil, the same word as the Aramaic "Messiah," which is said to mean, the anointed. If the name means one who travels much, it could not refer to the Jesus of two thousand years ago who spent his life in the small state called Palestine.

One of the main things that one must learn is to distinguish between the history of Jesus two thousand years ago and the prophecy of the Jesus 2,000 years ago often proves to be that of the Great Mahdi, the Restorer of the Kingdom of Peace on Earth who came to America in 1930 under the name of Mr. W. D. Fard. Later he'd admitted that he was Mr. Wallace Fard Muhammad, the One Whom the world had been looking for the come for the past 2,000 years. According to the Holy Qur'an's chapter and verse we have under discussion, the name Messiah, the meaning—fits that of the Mahdi more than any other man.

The Mahdi is a world traveler. He told me that he had traveled the world over and that he had visited North America for 20 years before making himself known to us, his people,

The History of Jesus' Birth, Death . . .

whom he came for. He had visited the Isle of the Pacific, Japan and China, Canada, Alaska, the North Pole, India, Pakistan, all of the Near East and Africa. He had studied the wild life in the jungles of Africa and learned the language of the birds. He could speak 16 languages and could write 10 of them. He visited every inhabited place on the earth and had pictured and extracted the language of the people on Mars and had a knowledge of all life in the universe. He could recite by heart the histories of the world as far back as 150,000 years and knew the beginning and end of all things.

The name Christ, Jesus, Jehovah, God, Allah and many other good names, rightly are His names and He came to give divine names to the whole of the 17 million so-called Negroes. Jesus was made an example for the Jews (Holy Qur'an 43:59). Jesus and his mother were made as a sign (23:50).

ARTICLE NO. 2 JULY 27, 1957
THE LAST MESSENGER - THE NEW BOOK

As we have the Bible's version of Jesus' history, I bring to you some of the history as given in the Holy Qur'an Sharrieff, translated into English by Maulvi Muhammad Ali, which is given for the purpose of clearing Jesus of false charges made by his enemies, the devil's writers.

Since the so-called Negroes' knowledge of Jesus came solely from the Bible, translated into English by the enemies of Jesus they will not accept anything other than what the devils teach, "Jesus and His mother a sign." (Holy Qur'an 23:50.) This is the best answer as yet given, for with such answer we have the key to this Man's birth, ministry and death-for that which serves as a sign is not the thing that it is a sign of, but only a sign of something to come or to be. As Moses birth, history and death as given in the Bible and Qur'an was a sign of what was to come, and I may add to the dislike of many Muslims, Muhammad's life and history was also a sign of that which was to come at the end of the World of the Infidels, be it understood.

He, who is the last of the Prophets, was clearly seen and made known to those Prophets before Him, and their life work reflects for us the life and work of the last Prophet, who is not really a prophet in the sense of the word, but rather an apostle or messenger, for He is the Answer and End of the Prophets. His call is unlike the others before him, for all of the Prophets before the last one had their call and mission through inspirations and visions for they saw not the Person of Allah (God) in reality—only in vision—but the last one is Chosen and Missioned directly from the mouth of Allah (God) in person at the end of the world.

He will also bring a Book for His people. A book that the present world has not as yet seen and the devils (infidels) may not see it nor touch it. It is not the present Holy Qur'an nor Bible, but a Book containing the guidance for the people in the Hereafter. Not of this world, therefore, it is carefully guarded from the eyes and ears of this world.

The last Messenger of Allah (God), his position to Allah (God) is not only like that of the moon to the Sun, which only reflects light in the absence of the Sun, but it's like that of the Planet Mercury, which is all but lost in the light of the Sun, and no other planet is between Mercury and the Sun. His message (the Truth) is like the Sun, which makes clear and distinct that which the Moon and Stars cannot. Can one say that of the present scriptures? The verse mentioned above (23:50) included Jesus' mother as also being a sign. Just what are the two a sign of? Look for the answer in this book.

6

ARTICLE NO. 3 AUGUST 3, 1957
THE BLACK STONE

Jesus, a sign; His mother, a sign; Muhammad and his birth, ministry, persecution and death, was also a sign of another one yet to come. I hope the readers of this book won't jump to conclusions before I have finished this history of Jesus and have shown the proof. You don't have to tell me—I know that it is no easy thing to change your belief in something that you were born in, but readers, just be intelligent enough to admit and agree on the Truth.

The birth of Musa (Moses) under the government of Pharaoh, who along with his people were enemies of Musa (Moses) and his people and who enslaved and killed Musa's people without justice, and the hiding and fleeing of Musa (Moses) from Pharaoh, are all a sign of the last Messenger. Jesus' birth, ministry and persecution, hated by Herod and the spiritual teachers of the Jews, as Pharaoh and his magicians hated Musa (Moses) and his followers. These two prophets histories show that they had no peace among the rulers and people to whom they were sent to guide and warn. The birth and death of Jesus meant the end of the rule and independence of the Jews, who rejected him as being a Prophet of Allah (God), which serves as a sign of what we may expect in the days of the Last One whom these two prophets, Musa and Isa (Moses and Jesus) prophesied would come in these last days or would be present with Allah (God) in person.

The Jews were expecting a prophet to be born in their midst (2,000 years) after the death of Musa (Moses) and know that one is to be raised up from the midst of their race just prior to the end (judgement) of their time.

They soon learned that Jesus was not that prophet. Muhammad, born in the Seventh Century after the death of

Jesus, the last sign of that last one coming with Allah (God) in the judgement or end of the world of devil's rule. Muhammad turned on the light (Islam) in the ancient house (Arab Nation) that had burned low since the time of Ibrahim (Abraham) and cleaned it up for the reception of a much brighter light of the Mahdi (Allah in the Person) and His people, which will come from the West out of the house of the infidels.

That last Messenger is the One chosen by the Mahdi, Allah (God) in person, in the last days whom the Mahdi finds lost and enslaved by the infidels in the West, of whom Abraham makes a sign with a small, unhewn black stone and set it in the Holy City of Mecca and veiled it over with a black veil which will not be unveiled and destroyed or discarded until he whom the sign represents is returned (the last Messenger and his followers).

Jesus spoke of the future of that stone in these word, "The stone which the builders rejected is become the head of the corner" (Mark 12:10). Muhammad found the stone out of place and had it put back into its proper place. This act of Muhammad shows that he was not the fulfiller of the sign which the stone represents, but rather a prototype of that which the stone represents. Moreover, Muhammad's replacing and repairing the sign (the stone) was a sign of the work of the Mahdi, who would, in His day, raise and put into proper place that which the stone now serves as a sign of.

Oh, that you would only understand the Scriptures. The Christians think the stone was Jesus. The Muslims think that it represents Muhammad 1,370 Years ago. The Prophets, for the saved people in the Hereafter, will love and praise Allah for him as this is the meaning of Muhammad, as the Muslim world respects and honors Muhammad today. There certainly is a surprise in store for both worlds (Islam and Christianity) in the revealing of this last One. Some of the religious scientist are already wise to it.

8

ARTICLE NO. 4 AUGUST 10, 1957
JESUS' HISTORY
FROM THE MOUTH OF ALLAH (GOD)

We know that most all white menfolk love to insult the black women; it is the nature of that race to destroy the black. So, he told his daughter (Mary) when she went out to care for the stock to wear his clothes, and he made her a beard out of a goat's beard to wear so that the filthy-thinking devils would think that it was he (the father of Mary).

After giving his daughter his instructions on how to protect herself against the insults of the devil , while he was visiting the new construction of a mosque, he took leave of the home for three days. After the father's departure, just at the time to feed the stock, there arose a great dust storm (dust cloud) which blotted out visibility. Under this darkness she became afraid to venture out, so while thinking of how the stock would be fed, she thought of Yusuf (Joseph), the only man that she could trust and the only one that she every loved.

She called him to come and go with her to feed her father's stock. Joseph came in answer to her call. On his arrival at the home of Mary, she showed him the old man's clothing and the goat's beard that she was to wear in her father's absence; but Joseph suggested to Mary to allow him to wear her father's clothes and the goat beard, and that she wear her own clothes as usual so that the infidels would think that he (Joseph) was the old man (Mary's father). So Joseph and Mary went together from that day on until the return of the old man three days later.

Mary asked Joseph to return after the first day, and on the second day she asked Joseph: "What about your wife, and what will she think of your coming here?" Joseph said, "I will tell her that I am working, building an infidel a house," as he (Joseph) was a carpenter. Mary said, "What if your wife says to you, "Where is the money?" This question Joseph had no answer for, so Mary gave Joseph some money to carry home with him (just in case). On the third day, the old man returned.

About three months later he began to notice his daughter taking on weight.

He asked her, "Mary, what have you been eating? You seem to be taking on weight."

She denied that there had been any change in her eating. The old man, her father, went on for a while and became very suspicious as he kept noticing Mary's continued increase in weight. Again he said to Mary: What has happened?" Mary denied not and said: "Father, do you remember when you left home to go to the building of the new mosque?" The father said, "Yes." She said: "Well on that day when you left a dust cloud arose and there was darkness; I was afraid to go out in such darkness to feed the stock, so I called Joseph to go with me, so he came and he did go with me that day and help feed the stock; and also the next day, until you came home."

Her father said: "Yes, it looks like he fed them plenty." And she said: "And this is why I am like this. I told you that I loved Joseph and while alone together, this is what happened. Now I have told you the truth. You may kill me or do as you please."

The father, listening to such confessions from his daughter felt real bad, for the law was the same then as it was in the time of Moses and the Jews and as it is today in the dominant Muslim world. If an unmarried girl is found to be pregnant out of wedlock, she must be killed and the killing falls to the lot of the parents.

As time passed he began to hate to look at Mary's pregnancy. He became sick over it and went to bed. He nearly pulled out all of his beard looking and worrying over what to do about his daughter.

So, at this time, and old prophetess (spiritual woman) met Joseph.

ARTICLE NO. 5 AUGUST 17, 1957
JESUS' HISTORY, BIRTH AND DEATH

When this old, spiritual woman met Joseph, she said to him: "Oh, Yusuf (Joseph), you are the father of Maryam's (Mary's) baby." This was a surprise to Joseph, to learn that this old woman knew of his secret visit to Mary, his boyhood and manhood sweetheart, and began to deny his guilt by saying: "No! No! I am not the father of Mary's child!" The old prophetess woman reaffirmed her charge and said: "Oh, yes, you are the father. I have only come to help you. Don't deny the child. He is the one prophesied in the Holy Qur'an as being the last prophet to the Jews. He is going to be a great man, and as long as His name lives, yours, as being His father, will live.

"I have come to teach you how to save and protect him from the Jew's planning; for the Jews will kill the child. They are expecting a prophet from Allah (God) to be born at this time, and if the child is not carefully protected, they will kill it."

Remember the Bible's saying: "Then Joseph, her husband (under the Jews' marital law), being a just man and not willing to make her a public example, was minded to put her away privily. While he thought on these things, behold, the angel of the Lord appeared unto him in a dream, saying: Joseph, thou son of David, fear not to take unto thee Mary, thy wife, for that which is conceived in her is of the Holy Ghost." (Matt. 1:19, 20). (The 18th verse of the above chapter of Matthew says, that Mary was espoused to Joseph before they came together.)

This word "espoused," according to the English language, when referred to man and woman—means engaged to be married, or to give in marriage, or to take up and support. In the case of Joseph and Mary, this seems to fit very well; for they were engaged to marry from childhood, but were never married. The child was conceived out of wedlock, for Joseph was already married to another woman and had six children by her, and these children, by his wife, are mentioned in Mark (3:31, 32). Of course, you will have to be careful about the readings, of what the Bible calls the Gospel of Jesus, because much of it is not authentic truth, and all Bible scholars will agree with me. Much of it is lost as that of the Torah (which they called the Old Testament) or the book of Moses. Of coarse, we know that the original Torah was one book and the Injil (Gospel) given to Jesus, was only one book. Added in and out of the truth, by the world writers, has caused so much misunderstanding of just what Allah (God) said and His prophets, that to correct it, Allah (God) has prepared a new book, altogether, for the lost found brother (the so-called Negroes). All the present scriptures, even the Holy Qur'an, have been touched by the hand of the enemies of the truth (the devils).

"Joseph, after hearing from the mouth of the old prophetess, that his son by Mary, was going to be a great man, a prophet, and the last one to the House of Israel (or the white race in general), he confessed that he was the father, regardless of the cost; which by the law, meant death for both him and Mary. But they were for—a sign of something that was to come— and, Allah (God) said that the old prophetess woman, told Joseph to go and confess to Mary's father, that you are the father of his daughter's unborn child. And, that the child is going to be the great and last prophet to the House of Israel (the Jews), and, that the Jews would try to kill the child—and, if you will allow me to take care of Mary, it won't happen. Now—I have told you the truth, so if you like, you can kill me. The old man (Mary's father) had the same thought as Joseph. Since the child is to be a prophet of Allah (God), as being the father of Mary, his name also would live; so, he agreed to let Joseph look after Mary."

Then Joseph asked the old man for the use of one of the stalls of his stock. Joseph took and filled the sides of the stall with straw and make a bed for Mary in the center. From the outside, the stall looked as though it was filled with straw. Joseph left a hole through which could feed Mary, and he was the nurse. In the dominate world of Islam, then and today, the parents teach both the boy and the girl, how to take care of the wife at childbirth. It is not like it is here in this world, where everything, along with yourself, is commercialized.

ARTICLE NO. 6 AUGUST 24, 1957
MARY FLEES TO EGYPT

Joseph rented one of those fast camels, put Mary and her baby on it, and said to the camel: "Take this woman to Cairo Egypt. Hurry! Hurry!" The camel went directly· to Cairo with Mary and her child, Jesus.

When Jesus was 4 years old, he began school, and at the age of 14 he was graduated. Jesus was very fast in learning (as Allah taught me). Jesus and his mother were Aboriginal Egyptians. This may be the reason Joseph sent them to Egypt—so that she would be among her own people, away from the Jews, whose intentions were to kill her child. The Aboriginal Egyptians are people of the black nation, and even the modern people of Egypt—in fact, all original Asiatic people are of the black nation. But the American so-called Negroes think that they do not have any people, except those who are in the jungles of Africa. The only people who are not members of the black nation are the white race.

At the time of Mary's flight to Egypt, the Jew's every intention was on finding and killing the child Jesus. But, once in Egypt the child was safe. Between the ages of 12 and 14, an old prophet came looking for Isa (Jesus). This old prophet had a knowledge of Jesus' presence and future life. He wanted to get to Jesus to inform him of just what he may expect, and how to protect himself from the evil intentions of his enemies (the Jews). He began going to the school at the time of dismissal to get a chance to meet Isa (Jesus).

When the boys started home, this old prophet would walk up and start looking among them for Jesus. On the

---

third day, he pretended to be looking for a certain address and the address was next door to the house where Jesus lived. He asked one of the boys if he knew where it was? While the boys were trying to think just where the place was—and another boy looked and said: "Here comes Isa (Jesus). He lives just next door to the number where you want to go. He will take you to it." The boy told Isa (Jesus) of the old man's desire to find the number, so Jesus said to the old man: "Yes, come with me, I know where it is. It is next door to where I live."

As Jesus and the old man walked on, alone, the old man asked Jesus what course was he studying. Jesus mentioned mathematics. The old man said to Jesus: "Yes, that is fine. I have a boy going to school taking the same course. Maybe you could help him." Jesus, who loved to teach someone, said: "Yes, I will teach your son." As they neared the address, the old man said to Jesus: "I am not looking for that address; it is you who I have been trying to get to for three days. I had intended to get to talk with you, if I had to fall down in front of you and let you stumble over me." He then said to Jesus: "Do you know who you are?" Jesus answered and said: "I don't know, but I believe I am going to be a great man." The old man said: "yes! You are the one who, the Holy Qur'an says, will be the last prophet to the Jews. I have come to teach you how to protect yourself. You will finish school and after finishing school, you will return to the Jew's land, and begin teaching them. If you don't know how to protect yourself, they will kill you. I will teach you how to tune in on them, so you can tell when they are planning to come and do you harm."

So, from that day, the old man began teaching Jesus in lessons, how to tune in on people and tell what they were thinking about. By Jesus already being a righteous boy, he learned in three lessons. The old man tested him and asked Jesus to tune in on him and talk with him. (It is not near as hard to receive a message as it is to send one out to a certain

person.) Jesus tuned in on the old man and greeted him.
The old man returned the greeting and said: "You are fine.
Now you are able to take care of yourself. This is what I
wanted to teach you. Now, you may go."

ARTICLE NO. 7 AUGUST 31, 1957
JESUS GIVES LIFE FOR TRUTH (ISLAM)

Jesus finally made the trip walking from Cairo, Egypt to Jerusalem, Palestine. Just how long it took him, I don't know. By having to stop and teach along the wayside, it must have taken quite some time. Nevertheless, on his arrival, he began teaching the Jews the religion of Islam. The Jews rejected Him and what he taught, except for a few.

Jesus, according to Allah (God), never was able to get over 35, or around that figure, to listen to him at one time. They hated Jesus and would refer to him as a liar, and that Moses was their prophet. They would call Jesus names that were so terrible, they can't be described in writing. There are any number of scripture in both the Bible and Holy Qur'an that Jesus was a prophet, sent to House of Israel alone. We have no scripture of him teaching anywhere else but among the Jews. He was not a universal prophet (not sent to the whole world). He made no attempt to teach the Arabs nor the blacks of Egypt or Africa. According to the history of his disciples, none of them carried Jesus' name and teachings into the countries of the black nation.

Paul, one of the greatest preachers and travelers of Jesus' followers, made no attempt to teach the black nation; nor travel into their countries. (I just can't see how the so-called Negroes think that he is their Saviour, when he didn't save the Jews to whom he was sent, and he has not saved the so-called Negroes from the slavery of white Americans). It is really a shame and a crime, worthy of death, for the devils to have tricked my people into the belief of Prophet Jesus being their God and Saviour:—a hearer of their prayers, and

---

18

at the same time, teaching them that they killed Jesus. It just doesn't make sense. May Allah burn such liars from the face of the earth, for deceiving my people whom they now kill and burn at will—because they know not their God—nor, even know themselves! It is sickness to listen to our poor people calling on Isa (Jesus) of 2,000 years ago, as though he were alive in their midst; and, they are really sincere. By my Allah (God), I will bring them into he knowledge of truth; and, to their God, Allah—or, die in the effort.

Break the head of falsehood. Confuse and bring to naught his lying missionaries, who have deceived my people with their lies of Allah and His Prophet Isa's (Jesus) birth and death; and, the scriptures of the prophets. (The so-called Negroes want to know why white people hide the truth from them—the answer is:—that they are the devils and know that one cannot be enslaved who knows the truth).

The Death of Jesus. Allah, the best knower, to whom be praised forever, who came in the person of Master W. F. Muhammad, said: "That, Jesus, after teaching and running from the devils for 22 years, learned from reading and study- ing the scripture, that he couldn't reform the infidel race. And that they had 2,000 years more to live to do their devil- ment, and deceive the nations of the earth. He decided to give his life for the truth (Islam): which he taught—and was rejected—for the 22 years of his life in Palestine.

One Saturday morning, between 9 and 10 o'clock, he came out on the streets of Jerusalem and saw a small group of people standing under an awning in front of a Jew's store, trying to shelter themselves from the rain. Jesus walked under the awning with the people and began teaching them. As his teaching began to interest the people, the store owner came out and told Jesus to leave for he was causing him the loss of sales. Jesus said to the Jew: "If you will allow me to continue to teach them here, while it is raining, I will make them buy something out of your store." The Jew agreed for

The History of Jesus' Birth, Death . . .

a while. But as time passed on, the Jew saw that the people were not buying as he thought they would. The Jew warned Jesus again to leave his store front. Jesus refused, because he had about 35 people, who had gathered to hear him. The Jew told Jesus: "I know who you are and if you don't leave my store, I will call the authorities."

ARTICLE NO. 8 SEPTEMBER 7, 1957
JESUS IS KILLED

After the Jew called the authorities to come and take Jesus, they sent two officers to arrest him. There was a reward of $1,500 if he were arrested and brought in alive— 2,500, in gold, if he were brought in dead. The two officers wanted this reward, so both ran to take Jesus and arrest him. They arrived almost at the same time. The two laid hands on Jesus and began quarreling over who was the first to lay his hands on Jesus. While arguing over whose prisoner Jesus actually was, Jesus asked the two officers if they would allow him to tell who touched him first. The two officers agreed. Jesus said: "The one on the right touched me about three-tenths of a second before the one on the left." The officer on the left accepted the decision and left.

Then Jesus and the other officer started walking down the street to turn him over to the authorities. While going on, the officer said to Jesus: "Since you came here to give yourself up to be killed, why not let me kill you and you will not feel it. But if I take you to them (the infidel Jews), they want to torture you—make you suffer. I will kill you in an instant and you will never feel death. Furthermore, I will get more for taking you there dead than alive. I am a poor man with a large family. Why not let me get the larger reward since you came to die?" Jesus agreed and said to the officer: "Come and do it." The officer took Jesus to an old deserted store front, which was boarded up to protect the store from possible stones, thrown by boys, that might break the glass. The officer said to Jesus: "Stand with your back against this store front and put your hands up." Jesus, being a brave man and ready to die, obeyed the officer and stretched forth his hands, like a cross (not on a cross, but made a cross of himself).

The officer drew a small sword-like knife from his side (which looks like the American hunting knife). Only this little sword is sharp, on both sides of the blade, to about two-thirds of its length. He plunged the sword through the heart of Jesus with such force that it went clear through and stuck itself into the boards that he was standing against (and left him as a crucifix). By Jesus having such strong nerves, his death was so instant that the blood stopped circulating at once. And Jesus was left stiff, with both arms out stretched in the same position as he put them when ordered by the officer. The authorities came and took him from the boards where the knife had pinned Jesus' body. When Joseph heard of his son Jesus' death, he came and got the body from the authorities. He secured some Egyptian embalmers to embalm the body to last for 10,000 years. Joseph wanted the body embalmed to last as long as the earth (petrified), but was not able to pay for such embalming. The Egyptian embalmers put the body into a glass tube filled with a certain chemical (known only to the Egyptian embalmers) that will keep one's body looking the same as when it died, that is if they get the body at a certain time, for many thousands of years—as long as no air is allowed to enter the tube that the body is in. They buried the body in the old city, Jerusalem.

His body lies in the tomb in such manner that it reflects in four different directions. This was done to keep the enemies from knowing in just what direction the real body is lying.

No Christian is allowed to see the body, unless they pay a price of $6,000 and must get a certificate from the Pope of Rome. The tomb is guarded by Muslims. When Christians are allowed to see Jesus' body, they are stripped of weapons, hand-cuffed behind their backs, and well-armed Muslim guards take them into the tomb. But, Muslims, the brothers of Jesus can go to see his body at any time without charge.

ARTICLE NO. 9 SEPTEMBER 21, 1957
JESUS BELONGED TO THE BLACK NATION

My people, who believe in Jesus as God and the Bible as the True Word of God on face value, have gone to the extreme in their belief, without the least knowledge of the true meanings of what they read and believe. You have been reading the history of Jesus in this article, as it was revealed to me by Allah (God) in person, whom you can't believe to have been God, because of your total blindness to the reality of God. (The truth hurts the guilty.)

Now that you believe that Jesus was a man of flesh and blood born of a woman as you and I were; and, that flesh was wounded by a knife that brought death to Jesus (and, the same wounded flesh came to life again and was seen going up in the sky of its own accord, until the view was shut out by clouds) that is the wrong way to believe, and understand that Bible story of Jesus. Nearly 75 per cent is referring to a future Jesus, coming at the end of the white races' time, to resurrect the mentally dead, lost members (so-called Negroes) of the tribe of Shabazz. This Jesus is now in the world.

Jesus and his mother made a sign of something to come; and, we are the end or fulfillment of that sign. "And we made the Son of Mary and his mother a sign." (Holy Qur'an 23:50). There are some who think that the sign refers only to the Jews, in the sense that Jesus was the last of the Prophets; not only to the Jews, but to the white race in general. We must not forget that Jesus was not a member of that race. Jesus belonged to the black nation.

In order to make the American so-called Negroes worship the devils, the American devils paint Jesus, God and the Angels white. Many of the so-called Negroes take these imaginary pictures as real; while there is not a real picture of Jesus, nor his disciples. The foolish American so-called Negroes have worshipped the devils (white race) all of their lives. Now, today, he will openly dispute with you that Jesus was a white man (a Jew); not taking the time to think, that if Jesus was a member of that white race, he would have been a devil. Again, Jesus would not have declared that the Jews were devils (John 8:44). The above chapter (8th Chapter: John) should convince the so-called Negroes, that the white race can't love and do good by them. They are not from the God of goodness, mercy and truth. (John 8:42) Jesus also condemned them in claiming Abraham to be their father (John 8:39).

The white races' work, their open hatred of us; their murdering and killing of you and me, themselves and the righteous proves beyond a shadow of a doubt, that they are the real devils. They actually love the making of war; persecuting and killing the so-called Negroes; and, worst of all— they make the frightened so-called Negroes help them war against whom they term to be their enemies; while they are the worst enemies of the Negroes, on earth. They openly tell the so-called Negroes that they will not give them equal justice with themselves. They will go to war against any few who attempt to give the Negroes justice.

24

The so-called Negroes see all of this going on against
them; and, yet love and desire to destroy themselves with
such enemies, rather than follow me to their own God and
people, with whom they will be given equal love and justice. They (so-called Negroes) even hate me for teaching the
truth, due to their ignorance of truth.

Jesus and his mother were a sign of the so-called Negroes' (the actual lost and found members of a chosen nation) history, among the devils, in the last days of the devils'
time on earth. The birth of Jesus (out of wedlock) was a
sign of the spiritual birth of the lost-found so-called Negroes
in North America; who are out of their own people and
country (out of the wedlock of unity) living and mixing their
blood with their real enemies, the devils, without knowledge. Yusuf (Joseph) and Mary's childhood love of each
other when old enough, was a sign of the love of Allah
(God) for the lost-found, so-called Negroes, at the end of
the devils' time (6,000 years). The visiting of Mary by Joseph, for three days under the cover of darkness, and in the
absence of the father, and under the disguise of Mary's father's
clothes and Joseph's wearing a goat's beard, was a sign of
how Allah (God), who is referred to in the name "Mahdi,"
would come under disguise Himself, in the flesh and clothes
of the devils, for three days (three years), to get to the lost-
found so-called Negroes and start them pregnating with the
truth through one of them, as a messenger, under a spiritual
darkness.

ARTICLE NO. 10 SEPTEMBER 28, 1957
RELIGION OF ISLAM
JESUS AND HIS MOTHER A SIGN
(HOLY QUR'AN 23:50)

My people (the so-called Negroes) should be real happy after reading the articles of truth in this paper that God has revealed to me, seeing that the salvation belongs to them and not to the Jews, as they have been made to believe.

It is a pity that they have been made so blind, deaf and dumb, to the extent that in order to make them believe the truth, Allah (God) will have to whip them into submission. That is why I am teaching them night and day, for the chastisement of Allah is to be feared even by the devils.

Beware, my people! Do not take what I am writing here in this paper as a joke or mockery. It is the divine truth, from the very mouth of God, and not a made-up story of myself. I have not the brains to think up such truth. I once was as dead as you are. Don't give men any credit for Allah's (God's) revelation of truth to me (even you who believe). Give praises to Allah, to Whom it is due, for I am only your brother and a sufferer with you, under the same. But if you would believe in Allah (God) as I do, though under your burden, you would feel it not.

So many of you are writing and asking almost the same questions. If you continue to read my articles you will find the answers to all of your questions.

Isa's (Jesus') birth and death (history of two thousand years ago, and his mother, are a direct sign of the history of the so-called Negroes here in America—the visit of Allah (God) and the raising of a Messenger from among them.

Why can't you understand?

The fleeing to Egypt of Mary and her baby, to be schooled
for His mission, is a sign of you (so-called Negroes). You
will be schooled there for twenty years. You will be taught
your language and many sciences of your people and your
beautiful universe that have never before been taught. You
will suffer here a little while longer, but, the joy that awaits
you will make you forget your suffering here overnight.

I see you on top and not on the bottom any more, for
Allah (God) Himself is doing this. Not you, nor I, nor our
kind—only by the orders of Allah. Fear not! Neither persecution or death will prevent your rise—those who believe.
Allah has said it. It didn't work in the past, nor is it going to
work today.

The Holy Qur'an and the Muslims have great respect for
Jesus, but not as God. He was only a prophet. "He (Jesus)
was naught but a servant, on whom we bestowed favor, and
we made him an example for the children of Israel." (Holy
Qur'an 43:59). Here he is mentioned as being an example
for Israel; and he was, in the way of a true Muslim (righteous). An example of a doer of righteousness and obedi-
ent to the law of Allah as Moses had given them.

Israel was never a doer of the law. The 57th verse of the
same chapter refers to what the Christian-believing black
people here (the so-called Negroes) will say to Muhammad.
"And when the son of Mary is mentioned as an example, lo!
the people (the so-called Negroes) raised a clamor (a loud
outcry; uproar; vehement expression of the general feeling)."

This is true of the shameful way the so-called Negroes
carry on over the name or mentioning of Jesus in churches
and public places, as though Jesus is present and looking
on. Poor people. I hope to bring you out of such ignorance

of Jesus. He was only a prophet and is dead like Moses and prophets of old. None can hear your prayers. You must pray to a living Jesus, or God, if you want your prayers answered.

Just be faithful and clamorous over the real Jesus of today; and you will surely go to Heaven with Him. The false doctrines of Jesus being God were introduced after His death.

And when Allah will say; "Oh, Jesus, Son of Mary, didst thou say to men: "Take Me and My mother for two gods besides Allah?" He will say: "Glory be to Thee; it was not for Me to say what I had no right to say, if I had said it, Thou wouldst indeed have known it. Thou knowest what is in my mind and I know what is in Thy mind. Surely Thou art the great knower of the unseen. I said to them naught save as Thou didst command Me. Serve Allah, my Lord and your Lord; and, I was a witness of them so long as I was among them, but when Thou didst cause Me to die, Thou wast the watcher over them, and Thou art witness of all things.

"If Thou chastise them, surely Thou art the mighty, the wise (Holy Qur'an 5:116-118)."

Remember the Bible teaches that Jesus was dependent upon His Father (God) in these words: "I can of Mine own self do nothing: as I hear, I judge: because I seek not mine own will, but the will of the Father which hath sent me." (St. John 5:30) God is not sent, nor does He depend on instructions from anyone. A prophet is sent with a message and is dependent on his sender for guidance. So was Jesus in every respect, even after His resurrection. He didn't claim to be God. "Touch me not: for I am not yet ascended to My Father." (John 20:17). "And now I am no more in the world, but these (His followers) are in the world, and I come to Thee, Holy Father, keep through Thine owe name, those whom Thou hast given me, that they may be one, as we are. While I was in the world. I kept them in Thy name." (John 17:11, 12).

28

Compare the above with the 5:117 of the Holy Qur'an. Jesus declared that He is no more in the world and cannot be witness of what His followers will do; nor be responsible for them after his death.

No other prophet is responsible for the people after he fulfills his mission to them or dies in the attempt. Study your book and understand the truth before you dispute with me. Jesus was only a prophet and is dead like Moses and the other old prophets. Pray to a living God and come follow me, and He will hear your prayers.

ARTICLE NO. 11 OCTOBER 5, 1957
**THE SO-CALLED NEGROES' SALVATION
IS THEIR OWN TRUE RELIGION, ISLAM,
UNDER THE GUIDANCE OF ALLAH (GOD),
TO WHOM BE PRAISE FOREVER**

The history of Jesus and His mother is a sign of the history of the so-called Negroes, who have been lost from their people for 400 years—who now are found and must be returned to their own; or else every Western (Christian) government will be brought to an aught by the Great God, Allah, under the name of Mr. W. F. Muhammad, "The Mighty Mahdi, the Son of Man," Allah in person.

As I have said and shown in my articles on Jesus' history most of Jesus' history 2,000 years ago is referring to an apostle in the last days, and not of the past. In several places, it is referring to the suffering of Allah (God) three and one-half years, trying to get to the so-called Negroes under disguise.

History repeats itself. The same race that hated Jesus 2,000 years ago hates Jesus' people (the so-called Negroes) today, and is casting them out. The limited knowledge that the so-called Negroes have of themselves and their enemies makes them think that the enemies' rejection of them is wrong, but is not.

It is really their salvation to be rejected by the devils. The wrong that the enemies are doing to you is that they won't let you go free. Indeed, they won't allow even Allah (God) to do so without war. They won't teach you the truth of self, God, devil or the true religion.

30

They persecute and kill you without justice. They put fear into you, and that fear makes you harmless like sheep before a pack of hungry, merciless wolves, who stay in your family after the so-called Negro women.

The poor people (so-called Negroes) and their foolish leaders (preachers) should visit and join onto your own, Islam from the cradle to the old man and woman leaning on a stick.

You shout and weep, pity poor Jesus' murder and death at the hands of His enemies 2,000 years ago, but is seems as though you should not cry nor weep over you own selves, being beaten and killed daily. Yet you say nothing nor do anything about it, but love the enemies.

The parable of us under the title "Lazarus laying at the rich man's gate" could not give a better type of the so-called American Negroes.

They just won't go for self, as long as the slave masters are rich and will allow you to be their servants and make rosy promises to you only to deceive you. But today is very serious for you and for them. Think well and wisely for your future.

Allah (God) and his religion, Islam, are your only friends. The white race is not able to help itself against Allah. So your believing and seeking a future in the race, today, is like one seeking shelter under a spider's web from a storm of hailstones.

The mother of Jesus well represents a messenger from among you, pregnation with a new world out of you.

Almighty God, Allah, is the Father and must protect the infant "baby nation" (the so-called Negroes) whom he is carrying.

Jesus, making a clay bird by the permission of Allah, the healing of the sick, giving sight to the blind, raising the dead, teaching the people what they should eat and what they shouldn't eat (Holy Qur'an 3:48) means one and the same thing. The work of the last apostle to the so-called Negroes, who are spiritually blind, deaf and dumb.

They are eating the wrong food and now being taught against the eating of poison foods by the Apostle of Allah. No such work was done among the devils 2,000 years ago. It was not necessary since the devils are not to be saved.

ARTICLE NO. 12 OCTOBER 12, 1957
JESUS: SIGN OF A FUTURE JESUS

Let me make myself clear to you, in regards to last week's article. I am not trying to condemn the history of Jesus as being false; but, rather am trying to put the meanings and signs, or miracles where they belong. That is, in the present so-called Negroes' history, and Jesus of today. Jesus and His parents were only a sign or prototype of that which was to come.

Of course, there are many student ministers in the theological seminary colleges, who probably know, or are learning, that most of what the Bible gives us of Jesus' history has got to be a future man and not one answering any such description of 2,000 years ago.

How could Jesus' birth and death 2,000 years ago serve as the price of sin and peace (reconciling God and the man of sin), of the world as the average Christian believe? The rejoicing angels at his birth; the mourning and directing angels at His tomb; the great earthquakes; the tense darkness; the seeing of resurrected saints; the going up to heaven in a cloud, as Matthew, Mark, Luke and John gives us in the gospel of Jesus?

It just can't be put in the past without disgracing the All Wise God's intelligent knowledge of the future. Let the poor so-called Negroes' minds relax for a few minutes, while reading this article, and use common sense. (1st) if Jesus were to have a flesh and blood body, He must be produced as we were, by the agency of man, who had flesh and blood. If God produces one other than by man, He breaks His own law. And, we could not be held responsible for breaking the same law (getting children out of wedlock). (2nd) The

---

world has never been without a righteous people on it. Could not God produce a son or prophet from a righteous couple as He had in the past? And, even as He did by Zacharias and his wife, to produce John, who was a little older than Jesus, according to the Bible (Luke 1:57).

Read the birth and death of Jesus as recorded in Matthew, Mark, Luke, and John. Think it over. Would God have permitted such thing to happen 2,000 years ago with such evil results following afterward? If Jesus' birth was to bring peace and goodwill to all mankind (Luke 2:14), how could He have prophesied of "Wars and rumors of wars, nations rising against nations, and the hatred of one another?" (Matthew 24:7-10). There have been more wars and more evil, since the birth and death of Jesus than ever before. Jesus didn't bring peace to the world, according to the Bible (Matthew 10:34). Elijah comes to unite the family and put them on the path of God, to bring about a union between man and God (Malachi 4:5,6).

According to the Bible, Jesus taught to "hate every member of the family, even the father and mother," (Luke 14:26). Even God said: "He loved one brother and hatred the other brother." (Romans 9:13). You, who preach that God is love and Jesus taught to love one another, should have consulted the translators of the Bible as to just why they charge God's and Jesus' teaching for a thing in one place and against it in another place.

Your Bible is poison, double crossing itself. Be careful how you understand it. We know what it means and where it belongs; but, since you are disbeliever in the truth and disputers without knowledge, we challenge you to prove your sayings by your book— if you have understanding of it.

You have two Jesus' histories, as I have said time and again; and, even an apostle's history of the last days, all under the name of Jesus, 2,000 years ago.

ARTICLE NO. 13 OCTOBER 19, 1957
JESUS, A SIGN AND EXAMPLE

I am so happy that Allah (God) has revealed to me the truth, believe it or not. Oh, you die-hard Christians, who are stubborn and proud against Allah (God) His word, and we who believe in Him and His word. My people are deaf, dumb, and blind; and gravely mislead by the enemy (devil). Use common sense, my people, and judge between the truth, which I am writing, and the false that was taught to you by the devils.

Jesus came as a sign of that which was to come. His birth, ministry, persecution and death were signs of the persecution and death, as I have written, of the future of you (the so-called Negroes) his people; and the persecution and rejection of the Great Mahdi (God in person) who has appeared among us in these last days of this race of devils, and has suffered the same. Jesus was an example of righteousness, a doer of the law of the Jews, which was given to them by Musa (Moses).

The world, looking for that Jesus to return, is not only ignorant but foolish. No one but a fool would believe that Jesus, who was here 2,000 years ago, is sitting in heaven waiting until his time to return and execute judgment. Tell the world the truth, and stop fooling yourself, if you know it; and, if you don't know it, step aside and stop trying to hinder us, who are telling the truth.

The Bible makes it a little too hard for the average reader to believe in Jesus as a prophet, or a man born by the agency of man, like you and I; though, never did God intend otherwise. The Holy Qur'an makes Jesus only a prophet of Allah

---

(God); and, that is all He was. It does not mention his father by name, though on many occasions, prophets and their great works of the past are mentioned without their father's names. There are many Muslims who think that His birth was without the agency of man. Most commentators, on the life and death of Jesus, disagree with the saying that, "Jesus dies on the cross, or was even murdered (killed)." They think that He traveled into India and died in Kashmir, but this is wrong. He did not go there, nor is that His tomb in Kashmir. It is only an old belief among those who actually did not know who, the Nabi (prophet) was, who came to Kashmir and died and was buried there, whom old settlers claimed came from the West. No real proof is shown that it was Jesus' body.

The scholars on the Holy Qur'an go to the extreme with the word "spirit" as the Christians do, especially in the case of Allah. My work is to bring you face to face with God, and to do away with spooky beliefs. The revealing of the spiritual word of Allah (God) to Mary or anyone, does not mean for you and me to believe that Jesus was born without the agency of man. The spirit or word of Allah (God) came to Moses' mother, to inform her about the future of her son (that He was a prophet). (Exodus 2:2). Both the Bible and Holy Qur'an seem to be very careful not to accuse Mary of fornication. Why? If she and her son were to be a sign for the nation, she should not be charged with fornication. (2nd) If the act was to serve as a lesson for us, that we should never allow two people who are in love with each other, to be alone together, in a place where there are no others, for nature has no self-control. That was the case of Mary and Joseph. They were childhood sweethearts, and wanted to be married when of age; but Mary's father objected to it. His objections could not destroy the love between the two. To this day, the Muslims keep boys and girls, men and women, from mixing freely together. Even the boy and girl courtships and marriages are controlled by their parents. There is no fornication, and very little or no divorce cases in

36

the dominant Muslim world. That is why Islam is hated by white Christian devils, because they are not allowed to mix with Muslim women; with their filthy, indecent hearts and winking blue eyes. "We breathed into her of our inspiration, and made her and her son a sign for the nations." (Holy Qur'an 21:91).

Regardless to the carefulness and chaste language of their scripture, used on Mary, having a baby out of wedlock, we can see through it all; after knowledge from Allah (God) in the person of Master Fard Muhammad (to whom be praised forever). In another chapter it mentions the spirit sent to Mary in the form of a man. "So she screened herself from them. Then we sent to her, our spirit, and it appeared to her as a well-made man." (Holy Qur'an 19:17).

ARTICLE NO. 14 NOVEMBER 2, 1957
NEGRO PREACHER WORST ENEMY

I am well aware of my disputers, who dispute without knowledge; and who are followers of the devils for certain privileges. They claim to be representatives of God and Jesus, whom they claim to be the Son of God, but are licensed, ordained and sent by the devils. (God-sent men are licensed, by the world). This class who love to be revered and honored by the people, whether God has any respect for them or not, are really agents for the slave masters (the devils). They are secret persecutors and murderers of the prophets of God, and will say: "If they had been their followers and would not have opposed them." Yet, they persecute me and my followers, and all who teach the truth, for the same things that the enemies of the prophets of old.

It was special privileges that Pharaoh offered the "Enchanters" to oppose Moses as being a liar. "He promised them that they would be drawn near to him," (Pharaoh). Holy Qur'an (7:113,114). It is the nearness (friendship) of the white race that the majority of the so-called Negro preachers seek and not the nearness, love, and friendship of God. They openly confess that in their position (licensed and missioned by the white race to preach according to their likings), they cannot preach the truth if that truth is against the white race. The followers' (church members') burdens are ever made grievous to carry, because of the love and fear of their enemies by the preachers. They call preaching the truth hatred.

Last week, this paper published the hatred of two preachers, of the truth that I am teaching my people in this book.

38

Namely, Rev. Joseph P. King, founder of the International Church of Chicago, Ill., and Rev. Benjamin F. Reid of Pittsburgh, Pa. Rev. Joseph P. King would like to question the source and extent of my knowledge of what I am teaching.

The source from which it springs, or fountain from which I drink, is the same source from which Noah, Abraham, Moses, and Jesus drank—Almighty Allah (God) of Whom you probably do not believe; as the disbelievers of the above mentioned prophets did not believe in those prophets' truth.

The early man (original man) knew the earth's revolutions; the circulation of blood or the existence of microbes. The only man or people who were late in acquiring such knowledge was the white race; who are the only late or new race we have on our planet. I agree with you on "adherence to the unknown is a throw-back to anyone or a nation." This is the number one hold back to the so-called American Negroes. Without the knowledge of self or anyone else, or the God of their salvation; and strictly adhering or following those who preach and represent a mystery God (unknown), but yet charges that mystery God with getting a son out of wedlock; and of waiting 4,000 years to produce His Son to give His made people (the Adamic race) the religion called Christianity, is the gravest charge that could be made against the All-Wise, All-Knowing, and All-Powerful God. And, they say: "The Beneficent God has taken to Himself a son." Certainly you have made an abominable assertion! The heavens may almost be rent thereat, and the earth cleave asunder, and the mountains fall down in pieces, That they (the Christians' preachers) ascribe a Son to the Beneficent God. And it is not worthy of the Beneficent God that He should take to Himself a Son. There is no one in the heavens and the earth, but will come to the Beneficent God as a servant." Holy Qur'an (19:88-93).

I bear witness with the above said, that an All-wise, All-powerful God does not need a son and He would get one as the Christians charge Him (out of wedlock), He could be charged with adultery. I repeat, "the white man's so-called Christianity is not only no good for the black man, but it is fast proving to be no good for the white race, who are the founders of that religion and not Jesus, as they would like for you to believe."

ARTICLE NO. 15 NOVEMBER 9, 1957
JESUS' HISTORY MISUNDERSTOOD
BY THE CHRISTIANS

The great misunderstanding over the Father and Sonship, birth and death of Jesus, is now being made understandable from the mouth of God in person; whose coming has brought light and truth to us who sit in darkness. The great arch-enemy of Allah and the righteous, the devil in person (Caucasian race), who has deceived us for 6,000 years, took us out of light of truth into darkness, and now Allah (God), by His grace and power, dispels the darkness and is making manifest this great enemy (the devil). The poor black man of America should rejoice and be glad for this divine truth of Jesus' birth, life, and death, as the real truth of it has never before been told.

Who is this Christ, and His Father that Jesus questioned the Pharisees about? Was Jesus referring to Himself, or another one as Christ? Or does, the above question of Jesus prove that He was the Christ, or that His Father was other than a man? By no means, for according to Joseph's dream (Matthew 1:20-21) concerning the birth of his son, his name was to be called Jesus. "And she shall bring forth a son, and thou shalt call His name Jesus, for He shall save his people from their sins." (Matthew 1:21). Did he save the Jews from their sins? They no doubt were not His people according to John (8:42-44). The Jews could not be saved from their sins if their father was the devil, for by nature they were sinners.

Joseph was the husband of Mary and the son of Jacob. In Joseph's dream, he was addressed by the angel as being the son of David (Matthew 1:16-20). Jesus is called "Jesus Christ," and "Emmanuel." Did the people in those days ever call Jesus "Emmanuel?"

Today, he is called "Jesus, and Christ the Son of God."
Since we have learned that He did not save the Jews from
their sins and that he denounced the Jews as being none
other than the devil; that He did not restore the independence of the Jews and did not bring peace to the world, nor
even to his disciples; nor did He put a stop to death, nor did
He destroy sickness from the people, but referred to the Son
of Man (Matthew 9:6) as having power on earth to forgive
sins. He could not have been referring to Himself as the
Son of Man who had such power, for He prophesied of the
coming of the Son of Man (Matthew 24:27,30,37,39,44).

The Bible is very questionable, but it can be, and is now
being understood, for God has revealed her hidden secrets
to me. Such things as "forgiving sins of a special people,
nor even as much as healing them; giving spiritual light;
resurrection of the dead; bringing peace and goodwill between man and man," could not have been in the days of
Jesus 2,000 years ago. Think over it! "Angels coming from
heaven to bear witness that he is the One to set up the
Kingdom of Peace"; and yet, when He began His ministry,
He was dependent on His Father for help, and prophesied
of another; the coming of the Son of Man, who would be
self-independent, having power to restore the Kingdom of
Peace on earth and to destroy those who had destroyed the
peace and brotherhood of His people."

Learn, my dear readers, that the prophesied Son of Man,
is Almighty God. And, the Christ, long looked for, has come
in the person of Master Fard Muhammad, as it is written;
"without observation," or "as a thief in the night." The work
that I am doing in the midst of you bears witness of His
presence; for by no means do I have power of myself to
give life to the spiritually dead (so-called Negroes) except it
be from Him. You have had and still have the wrong understanding of the Bible. According to the Bible, David in his
palms, prophesied that he heard the Lord say unto his lord,
"Sit on my right hand until I make thine enemies thy foot-

stool." This prophesy cannot refer to Jesus of 2,000 years ago, for the Jews have not been made Jesus' footstool; which means being brought into submission, and Jesus being made the victor or their conqueror. The "Lord" that David refers to is Almighty Allah (God), and "his lord" is none other than the Great Prophet, coming just prior to the end of the world, whom the wicked will attack to do to Him what they did to the prophets of old. But Allah (God) will come to his aid. David, also being a prophet, saw the last prophet to be much greater than himself and calls him "his Lord." Let the so-called Negroes rejoice for they are the ones whose sins will be forgiven and shall be saved.

ARTICLE NO. 16, November 16, 1957
THE COMING AND PRESENCE OF
"THE SON OF MAN"

"For as the lightning cometh out of the East, and shineth even unto the West, so shall also the coming of the Son of Man be." (Matthew 24:27.)

My greatest and only desire is: to bring true understanding of the word of God, His prophets and the scriptures which the prophets were sent with, pertaining to the lost-found people (the American so-called Negroes) of God, and the judgement of the world.

You must forget about ever seeing the return of Jesus, who was here two thousand years ago. Set your heart on seeing the One that He prophesied would come at the end of the present world's time (the white race's time). He is called the "Son of Man," the "Christ," the "Comforter." You are really foolish to be looking to see the return of the Prophet Jesus. It is the same as looking for the return of Abraham, Moses and Muhammad. All of these prophets prophesied the coming of Allah or one with equal power under many names. You must remember that Jesus could not have been referring to himself as returning to the people in the last days. He prophesied of another's coming who was much greater than he. Jesus even acknowledged that he did not know when the hour would come in these words:

"But of that day and hour knoweth no man, no, not the angels of heaven, by my Father only." (Matthew 24:36).

If He were the one to return at the end of the world, surely He would have known the time of His return-the

knowledge of the hour. But he left himself out of that knowledge and placed it where it belonged, as all the others -
prophets - had done. No prophet has been able to tell us
the hour of the judgement. None but He, The Great, All
Wise God-Allah. He is called the "Son of Man," the "Mahdi,"
the "Christ." The prophets, Jesus included, could only fore-
tell those things which would serve as signs - signs that
would precede such a Great One's coming to judge the world.
The knowledge of the hour of judgement is with the Execu-
tor only.

The prophets teach us to let the past judgement of people,
their cities and their warner serve as a lesson, or sign, of the
last judgment and its warners. Noah did not know the hour
of the flood. Lot did not know the hour of Sodom and
Gomorrah until the Executors had arrived, and Jesus prophesied (Matthew 24:37-39) that: "It will be the same in the
last judgement of the world of Satan." You have gone astray
because of your misunderstanding of the scripture, the
Prophet Jesus, and the coming of God to judge the world.
My corrections are not accepted.

Your misunderstanding and misinterpretations of it are
really the joy of the devils. For it is the devils' desire to keep
the so-called Negroes ignorant to the truth of God until they
see it with their eyes. The truth of God is the salvation and
freedom of the so-called Negroes, from the devils' power
over them, and the universal destruction of the devils' power.
Can you blame them? No! Blame yourself for being so
foolish to allow the devils to fool you in not accepting the
truth after it comes to you.

The devils have tried to deceive the people all over the
planet earth with Christianity; that God, the Father, Jesus the
Son, the Holy Ghost - the three Gods into One God; the
resurrection of the son and his return to judge the world, or,
that the son is in some place above the Earth, sitting on the
right hand side of the Father, waiting until the Father makes
His enemies His footstool.

The History of Jesus' Birth, Death . . .

The period of waiting is 2,000 years. Yet he died for the Father to save his enemies (the whole world of sinners).

My friends, use a bit of common sense. First: Could a wonderful flesh and blood body, made of the essence of our earth last 2,000 years on the earth, or, off the earth, without being healed? Second: Where exists such a heaven, off the earth, that flesh and blood cannot enter heaven? (Corinthians 15:50.)

Flesh and blood cannot survive without that of which it is made-the earth. Jesus' prophesy of the coming of the Son of Man is very clear, if you rightly understand. First: This removes all doubts in whom we should expect to execute judgment, for if man is to be judged and rewarded according to his actions, who could be justified in sitting as judge of man's doings but another man? How could a spirit be our judge when we cannot see a spirit? And, ever since life was created, life has had spirit. For without life there is no spirit. But the Bible teaches that God will be seen on the Day of judgment. Not only the righteous will see Him, but even His enemies shall see Him.

ARTICLE NO. 17, November 23, 1957
THE COMING OF THE SON OF MAN-
THE GREAT MAHDI

"And shall appear the sign of the Son of Man in Heaven; and then shall all the tribes of the earth mourn, and they shall see the Son of Man coming in the clouds of Heaven with power and great glory." (Matthew 24:30). The final battle between God and the devils will be decided in the skies. The devils see Him and His power in Heaven and Earth. The nations of the West are in great pain trying to form their defense. Now is a very serious time on our planet and it will continue to be until the powers of this world are destroyed. The hour of this world has arrived. How will the Son of man win the battle against this world's use of Space weapons?

As we now realize from my article of last week, Jesus' prophecy of a man (Son of Man) coming at the end of the white race's (Devil's or the Man of Sin's) time which was up in 1914 makes it very clear as to what we should expect. It is a man, the son of another man, not a spirit, as we all are sons of men. On that day, a Son of Man will sit to judge men according to their works. Who is the Father of this Son, coming to judge the world? (I will tell you soon in this article). Is His father of flesh and blood, or is He a "spirit"? Where is this Son coming from? Prophet Jesus said: "He will come from the East" (Matthew 24:27) from the land and people of Islam, where all of the former prophets came from. Jesus compared His coming as "the lightning." Of course, lightning cannot be seen nor heard at a great distance.

"The actual light (the Truth) which "shineth out of the East and shineth even unto the West," is our day sun. But the Son of Man's coming is like both the lightning and our day sun. His work of the resurrection of the mentally dead so-called Negroes, and judgment between truth and falsehood, is compared with lightning-on an instant. His swiftness in condemning the falsehood is like the sudden flash of lightening in a dark place (America is that dark place), where the darkness has blinded the people so that they cannot find the "right way" out. The sudden "flash of lightning" enables them to see that they are off from the "right path." They walk a few steps towards the "right way," but soon have to stop and wait for another bright flash. What they actually need is the light of the Sun (God in person), that they may clearly see their way. The lightning does more than flash a light. It is also destructive, striking whom Allah pleases of property and lives. The brightness of its flashes almost blinds the eyes.

So it is with the coming of the Son of Man, with the Truth, to cast it against falsehood-that it break the head. Just a little hint of it makes the falsehood begin looking guilty and seeking cover from the brightness of the Truth. Sometimes lightning serves as a warning of an approaching storm. So does Allah (God) warn us by sending His messengers with Truth, before the approaching destruction of a people to whom chastisement is justly due. They come flashing the Truth in the midst of the spiritually darkened people. Those who love spiritual darkness will close their eyes to the flash of Truth, like lightning, from pointing out to them the "right way," thus blinding themselves from the knowledge of the approaching destruction of the storm of Allah (God), and are destroyed. "As the destruction of the storm of Allah (God), and are destroyed. "As the lightning cometh out of the East so shall the coming of the Son of Man be."

Let us reflect on this prophecy from the direction in which this Son shall come, "out of the East." If He is to come from the East, to chastise or destroy that of the West, then He must be pleased with the East. The dominant religion of the East is Islam. The holy religious teachings of all the prophets, from Adam to Muhammad, was none other than Islam (Holy Qur'an 4:163). They all were of the East and came from that direction with the light of Truth and shone toward the old wicked darkness of the West. But the West has ever closed its eyes and stopped up its ears against the Truth (Islam) and persecutes it, thus making it necessary for the coming of the Son of Man (the Great Mahdi) - God in person.

Being the end of the signs, in His person, He dispels falsehood with Truth as the sun dispels night on its rising from the East. Why should the tribes of the earth mourn because of the coming of the Son of Man, instead of rejoicing?

ARTICLE NO. 18, November 30, 1957
**THE COMING OF THE SON OF MAN:
WILL YOU BE THE WINNER?**

The non-Muslim world cannot win a war against the Son of Man (God in person), with outer space weapons or inner space. It does not matter for He has power over everything-the forces of nature and even our brains. He turns them to thinking and doing that which pleases Him. The great waste of money to build your defense against Him or the third world war is useless. You don't need navies, ground forces air forces or standing armies to fight the last war. What America Needs to win with is: freedom and equal justice to her slaves (the so-called Negroes). This injustice to her slaves is the real cause of this final war. Give them up to return to their own, or divide with them the country that you took from their people (the Red Indians) which they have helped you to build up and maintain with their sweat and blood for 400 years. They even give all their brain power to you. They help you kill anyone that you say is your enemy, even if it is their own brother or your own brother. What have you given them for their own labor and lives?

Is it just a job or labor for you? You hunt them and shoot them down like wild game; burn them; castrate them; they are counted as sheep for the slaughter-all who seek justice. You have continuously persecuted me and my poor followers for 25 years. Both fathers and sons are sent to prison. Just because we believe in justice and teach our brethren the same, we are imprisoned from three to five years and forced to eat the poison and divinely prohibited flesh of the filthy swine in our food, to your joy.

You set your agents around and about our meeting places where we are trying to serve the God of our fathers, to frighten our poor, blind, deaf and dumb people away from hearing and believing in the truth. With 48 states, which equal approximately three million square miles; with billions of dollars in gold buried and rusting, which we helped to get for you, yet none is ours; not the tiniest nor the most worthless state of yours have you offered your loyal slaves. Nor even to one square mile for their 400 years of labor. Shall you be the winner in a third world war? The God of Justice (the Son of Man, the Great Mahdi) shall be the winner. He is on the side of the so-called Negroes, to free them from you, their killers. As it is written, "Shall the prey be taken from the mighty or the lawful captives delivered? But thus said the Lord, even the captives of the mighty shall be taken away and the prey of the terrible shall be delivered; for I will contend with him that contend with thee. I will feed them that oppress thee with their own flesh, and they shall be drunken with their own blood. As with sweet wine, and all flesh shall know that I the Lord am thy Saviour, and thy Redeemer." (Isaiah 49:24-26.)

White Christian America has been so busy trying to keep her slaves (the so-called Negroes) under her foot, sitting, watching, spying on them to prevent them from knowing the truth of this day of our salvation, she has failed to see and learn the strength and power of her enemies. She has boasted that she could police the world and has come pretty near doing so, but failed to see the "bear" behind the tree and the "lion" in the thicket. The sky over her is being filled with her enemies' arms which can be seen with the naked eye. Her scientists are troubled and at their wits end to find time to make ready, as it is written: "I have set the point of the sword against all their gates, that their heart may faint, and their ruins be multiplied. Ah! It is made bright. It is wrapped up for the slaughter." (Ezekiel 21:15)

Answer: "For the tidings: because it cometh, and every heart shall melt and all hand shall be feeble and every spirit shall faint and all knees shall be weak as water," (Ezekiel 21:7.)

ARTICLE NO. 19, December 7, 1957
THE COMING OF THE SON OF MAN- THE INFIDELS (ANTI-CHRISTS) ARE ANGRY

Who is His father if God is not His Father? God is His Father, but the Father is also a man. You have heard of old that God prepared a body, the expected Son of Man; Jesus is a special prepared man to do a work of redeeming the lost sheep (the so-called Negroes). He had to have a body that would be part of each side (black and white), half and half. Therefore, being born or made from both people, He is able to go among both black and white without being discovered or recognized.

This He has done in the person of Master W.F. Muhammad, the man who was made by His Father to go and search for the lost members of the Tribe Shabaaz though you find them among the infidels, return them to their own. Master W. F. Muhammad is that Son of Man that the world has been looking for to come for 2,000 years, seeking to save that which was lost.

There are no historical records that there was ever a people lost from each other for 400 years other than we, the so-called Negroes. We have been so long separated from each other that we have lost the knowledge of each other. Even today the white American slave-masters are ever on the watch to keep out any Asiatic influence that might come among the so-called Negroes to teach them the truth. They are our real open enemies. This is no secret. The Son of Man is after the so-called Negroes to sit them in Heaven and His enemies in Hell. After His conquest of the black nation's enemies, the world will know and recognize Him (Allah) to be God alone.

There is no problem today that is as hard to solve as the problem of uniting the American so-called Negroes. They are like a dead man totally without life. The have lost all love of self and kind and have gone all out in loving their enemies (the devils). They do not seem to want any God to do anything like blessing them unless that God blesses their enemies, too. Fear of their enemies is the real cause.

The time is now ripe that they should have no fear, only the fear of Allah, who is in person among them to save them from their enemies. By all means, they must be separated from the white race (the devils), in order that the scripture might be fulfilled. "For I will take you from among the heathen and gather you out of all countries and will bring you into your own land." (Ezekiel 36:24). The so-called Negroes have no home (country) that they can call their own. They have helped the white race (the devils) to own a free country, but they have nothing for themselves. This is the purpose of His coming; to give everyone that which is rightfully theirs. The son of Man (the Great Mahdi, God in person) has power over all things. You cannot find a defense against Him in war. Your weapons mean nothing. The powers of Heaven and earth today will be ordered to fight on the side of the Mahdi (Son of Man) against His enemies. He is the friend of the so-called Negroes and not of white people. His purpose is to take the so- called Negroes and kill their enemies, although many of us will suffer from persecution and hunger. But the good end is for those of you who will find hold fast to Allah and His religion, Islam. They (the devils) are now planning many tricks to keep the Negroes here with them to suffer the fire of hell which they (the devils) cannot escape. Fly to Allah! come, follow me. Although I may look insignificant to you, you will find salvation with us. The white race is excited and cannot think rightly for themselves. The so-called Negroes, Muslims, in their midst are a shelter but little do they know it.

ARTICLE NO. 20, December 14, 1957
THE COMING OF THE SON OF MAN
(THE GREAT MAHDI)
AND THE GREAT DECISIVE BATTLE IN THE SKY

The final war between Allah (God) and the devils is dangerously close. The very least friction can bring it into action within minutes. There is no such thing as getting ready for this most terrible and dreadful war; they are ready! Preparation for battles between man and man or nations have been made and carried out on land and water for the past six thousand years. But, man now has become very wise and knows many secret elements of power from the nature world which make the old battles with swords and bow and arrows look like child's play.

Since 1914, which was the end of the time given for the devils (white race) to rule the original people (black nation), man has been preparing for a final showdown in the skies. He has made a remarkable advancement in everything pertaining to a deadly destructive war in the sky. But Allah, the best of planners, having a perfect knowledge of His enemies, prepared for their destruction long ago, even before they were created. Thanks to Allah, to whom be praised forever, who came in the flesh and the blood, and for more than seventy years He has been making Himself ready for the final war.

Allah, to Whom be Praised, came in the person of Master W. F. Muhammad; the Great Mahdi expected by the Muslims and the anti-Christs (the devils) under the names: Jesus Christ, Messiah, God, Lord, Jehovah, the last (Jehovah) and the Christ. These meanings are good and befitting as titles, but the meaning of His name "Mahdi," as mentioned in the

Holy Qur'an Sharrieff is better. All, of these names refer to Him. His name, FARD MUHAMMAD, is beautiful in its meaning. He must bring an end to war, and the only way to end war between man and man is to destroy the war-maker (the trouble maker).

According to the history of the white race (devils), they are guilty of making trouble; causing war among the people and themselves ever since they have been on our planet Earth. So the God of righteousness has found them disagreeable to live with in peace and has decided to remove them from the face of the earth. God does not have to tell us that they are disagreeable to live with in peace; we already know it, for we are the victims of these trouble makers. Allah will fight this war for the sake of His People (the black people), and especially for the American so-called Negroes. As I have said time and again, we, the so-called American Negroes, will be the lucky ones. We are Allah's choice to give life and we will be put on top of civilization.

Read your "poison book" (the Bible). What does your book say concerning the preparation of God against the devil? Take a look at Ezekiel's vision of it, 595 B.C. "Now it came to pass in the thirtieth year, in the fourth month, in the fifth day of the month, as I was among the captives by the river of Chebar, that the heavens were open and I saw visions of God. Now as I beheld the living creatures, behold one wheel upon the earth by the living creatures, with his four faces. As for their rings, they were so high that they were dreadful; and their rings were full of eyes around about them four." (Chapter 1: 1, 2, 15, 18.)

It was on the fourth of July, 1930, when the Great Mahdi, Allah, in person, made His appearance among us.

ARTICLE NO. 21, December 21, 1957
THE GREAT DECISIVE BATTLE IN THE SKY
THE SON OF MAN (GOD IN PERSON)
AND THE DEVILS

THE vision of Ezekiel's wheel in a wheel is true, if understood. There is a similar wheel in the sky today which well answers the description of Ezekiel's vision. This wheel corresponds in a way with the spheres of spheres called the universe. The Maker of the universe is Allah (God), the Father of the black nation which includes the brown, yellow and red people.

The great wheel which many of us see in the sky today is not so much of a wheel, but rather a plane made like a wheel. This wheel-like plane was never before seen. You cannot build one like it and get the same results. Your brains are limited. If you would build one to look like it, you could not get if up off the earth into outer space.

MAYBE I SHOULD not say the wheel is similar to Ezekiel's vision of a wheel, but that Ezekiel's wheel has become a reality. His vision of the wheel included hints on the great wisdom of Almighty God, Allah; that really He is the Maker of the universe, and reveals just where and how the decisive battle would take place (in the sky).

When guns and shells took the place of the sword, man's best defense against such weapons was a trench, poison gas and liquid fire to bring him out. Today, he has left the surface for the sky to destroy his enemy by dropping bombs. All this was known in the days of Ezekiel, and God revealed to him through Ezekiel that we may know what to expect at the end of this world.

56

The originator and his people (the original black people) are supremely wise. Today we see the white race preparing for the sky battle determine who shall remain on this earth, black or white. In the battle between God and the disbelievers in the days of Noah, the victor's weapon was water. He used fire in the case of Sodom and Gomorrah. In the battle against Pharaoh, He used 10 different weapons, which included fire and water, hailstones, great armies of the insect world and droughts.

The Holy Qur'an says: "The chastisement of Pharaoh was like that which God would use against His enemies in the last days." Throughout the Bible and Holy Qur'an teachings on the judgment and destruction of the enemies, fire will be used as the last weapon. The earth's greatest arms are fire and water. The whole of its atmosphere is made up of fire and water and gases. It serves as a protected coat of arms against any falling fragments from her neighbors. Ezekiel saw wheels in the middle of a wheel. This is true; there are wheels in the wheel.

THE PRESENT wheel shaped plane known as the mother of planes, is one-half mile by half mile and is the largest man-made object in the sky; a small human planet made for the purpose to destroy the present world of the enemies of Allah. The cost to build such a plane is staggering! The finest brains were used to build it. She is capable of staying in outer space six to 12 months at a time without coming into the earth's gravity. It carries 1,500 bombing planes and the deadliest explosives; the type used in bringing up mountains on the earth. The very same method is to be used in the destruction of this world.

ARTICLE NO. 22, December 28, 1957
THE GREAT DECISIVE BATTLE IN THE SKY BETWEEN GOD AND THE DEVILS

And there shall be signs in the sun and in the moon and in the stars, and upon the earth distress of nations, with perplexity; the sea and the waves roaring; men's hearts failing them for fear; and for looking after those things which are coming on the earth; for the powers of the heaven shall be shaken. They see the Son of Man coming in a cloud with power and great glory" (St. Luke 21:25-27).

You will bear me witness that we are living in such time as mentioned in the above prophecy-signs in the sun and in the moon. The phenomenon going on in the sun and its family of planets testifies to the truth that something of the greatest magnitude is about to take place. The final war or battle between God and the devils in the sky.

Allah (God) who has power over all things, is bringing the powers of the sun, moon, and stars into display against His enemies. The fire of the sun to scorch and burn men and the vegetation and to dry up the waters. The moon will eclipse her light to bring darkness upon man and upon all living, to disrupt with her waves all air communications. The magnetic powers of the moon will bring about such tidal waves of seas and oceans as man has never witnessed before; the sea and the waves roaring.

As men's hearts fail them with fear at sea looking upon great tidal waves coming toward them like mountains, they also shall see such a great display of power from Allah (God) in the sky that their hearts will fail. Great earthquakes never

58

felt before since man was upon the earth will take place, says the Bible and Holy Qur'an. The Holy Qur'an says: "There will not be one city left that will not be leveled to the ground." Using this force against the enemies of Allah will make it impossible for them to survive.

This is known to this world, but why are they trying to build up a defense against God? It is useless. America has it coming. Look how she has and still is mistreating her freed slaves (so-called Negroes). In the South, they are beating and killing the so-called Negro boys about their own so-called Negro girls. Neither the Negro girl nor the Negro boy can walk free at night in certain parts without being attacked, according to a certain worker's paper; yet the foolish Negro preachers and leaders want social equality with these, their enemies. The great distress of nations spoken or prophesied of coming in the above chapter and verses is now going on. Confusion, confusion all over the Western world today.

Should not it make you think that there is something of a very great importance going on among the nations of earth just to see the President leave his own country to visit another country during his tenure of office? They see the end of their world and they see the signs of the Son of Man coming in the sky with power and great glory (the great Ezekiel's wheel and the unity of the Muslim world and the distress of nations).

The nations are so well armed today that one nation fears the attacking of the other, lest he set off the whole third world war. THe so-called Negroes must awaken before it is too late. They think the white man's Christianity will save them regardless to what, and they are gravely mistaken. They must know that the white man's religion is not from God nor from Jesus or any other of the prophets. It is controlled by the white race and not by Almighty Allah (God).

"The near event draws nigh, there shall be none besides Allah to remove it. Do you wonder at this announcement? And will you laugh and not weep? While you sport and play, so make obeisance to Allah and serve Him" (Holy Qur'an 53:57,58,59,60). Let us remember another Qur'an saying: "None disputes concerning the communications of Allah (God) but those who disbelieve, therefore let not their going to and fro in the cities deceive you. The people of Noah and the parties after them rejected (prophets) before them, and every nation purposed against their Apostle to destroy him, and they disputed by means of the falsehood that they might thereby render null the truth. Therefore I destroyed them: how was then my retribution and thus did the word of you Lord prove true against those who disbelieved that they are the inmates of the fire (Holy Qur'an 40:4-6).

Hurry and join onto your own kind. The time of this world is at hand.

Subscribe!

To The Fastest Growing Newspaper Available, Which Gives It Straight, Regardless of Whom Or What!

(see membership info.)

Dedicated To
Elijah Muhammad
Last Messenger of Allah

In The Name of Allah, the Master Fard Muhammad

MESSAGE TO THE BLACKMAN

Volume 3 No. 6   September/October 1996   Donation $1.00

PLAYING WITH STEEL

GANGS: The Baggage of White Rule

As the scholars examine this seemingly new phenomena, they must determine if it's actually a new "American bruise" or just the pus ozzing from an old European "infection"

By Minister Nasir Hakim, Pg. 3

Are The Followers of Messenger Elijah Muhammad Practicing Shirk (Polytheism)? Pg. 6

COMING SOON

Elijah Muhammad Messenger of Allah

Autobiographically Authoritative

See Pg. 5

Mail Surveillance: Sources & Methods Pg. 12

Messenger Elijah Muhammad Propagation Society

(MEMPS) Humbly Invites You To Become A Valued Member!

The **MEMPS MEMBERSHIP** is an effective cost cutting way to invest in various forms of Messenger Elijah Muhammad's works.

These works consist of an extensive amount of lectures, public meetings, national and international interviews, radio and television broadcasts, annual conventions, temple dedications, and various table talks.

Much of these works were not available to the public at the time they were produced. Additionally, with the limited forms of media at that time, reproduction of these works were not as easy as it is today. Most of these works were lifted or transferred from reel to reel recorder and much of the video footage was originally on 35mm film, which was very common and accessible in those days. The public did not have nearly as many reel to reel recorders and 35mm film projectors as they now have of audio cassette players and Video Cassette Recorders (VCR's).

The same could stand as a reason why many who actually was in the Nation of Islam, didn't know much of this information from the Messenger existed; consequently, they have come to see that even they may still need clarity on various points and positions Elijah Muhammad, Messenger of Allah taught about.

Our objective is to deliver these truths of the Messenger to as many of our people who seeks it. Regardless of their respective understanding of the teachings and the ways they are expressing them, a membership, which makes these great works easy to get a very low cost, was highly necessary. We are confident that those who seek these words of the Messenger will greatly benefit.

We have the largest accessible collection of Messenger Elijah Muhammad's works in the world!

Not only is our collection in hard copy, but we have, to date, the ONLY computerized database of Elijah Muhammad's teachings in the world!

Our publications of Elijah Muhammad are drawn from hundreds of lectures, articles, video & audio tapes which makes them highly comprehensive and unmatched since Muhammad's Temple No. 2 publishing.

Our database will be online (Fax) soon along with the availability of the 1st encyclopedia anthology of his works!

Benefits:

✦ **FREE 1 YEAR SUBCRIPTION TO MESSAGE TO THE BLACKMAN**
Message To The Blackman is a hard hitting tabloid that deals with many of different perspectives of issues for and about Black people. Our "slant" is that of critical analysis. Many have chosen themselves as leaders of our people, but how many are actually qualified? Are those who are qualified getting the attention warranted? In addition to feature writing, you can expect a scope of Business, Diet, Education, Politics, Local, National and International news.

✦ **FREE BUSINESS LISTING IN MTTB**
When traveling, how convenient it would be to find the kinds of quality products and services that you want while simultaneously recycling those dollars.

✦ **FREE PREPUBLISHING DISCOUNTS**
We will are always working on new books which are designed and compiled solely from the database of Messenger Elijah Muhammad. We will forward our members a discount off the publisher's price, and the member can use their member "discount off book" to realize even more savings!

✦ **20% DISCOUNT ON AUDIO TAPES**
Regardless where you may find audio tapes by Elijah Muhammad, you will pay at least $8 to $10 for a single 30 minute radio broadcast. Why bother? Our tapes are by far the best quality you can buy, because of our exclusive filtering, noise reduction process we subject all our tapes to. Now you can get good quality at a good low price.

✦ **20% DISCOUNT ON VIDEO TAPES**
Our list of video are of good quality. The events on the videos are from lectures and conventions which are rare and hard to come by.

✦ **20% DISCOUNT ON PHOTOGRAPHS**
Some of these photos and prints are rare photos, all of which are of Messenger Elijah Muhammad. The majority are black and white; however, we have color and duo-tones.

✦ **20% DISCOUNT ON ALL BOOKS BY ELIJAH MUHAMMAD**
We carry the classics such as Message To The Blackman In America, The Fall of America, How To Eat To Live - Books 1&2, Our Saviour Has Arrived, The Supreme Wisdom - Vol. 1 & 2, The Flag of Islam. NEW BOOKS: The Mother Plane, 100 Answers To The Most Uncommon 100 Questions, Jesus' History-His Birth & Death, History of the Nation of Islam, The Time & The Judgement, The Secrets of Freemasonry, Christianity vs Islam. (All perfect bound. gloss covered books) AND YES - THE TRUE HISTORY OF MASTER FARD MUHAMMAD & THE TRUE HISTORY OF ELIJAH MUHAMMAD. AUTOBIOGRAPHICALLY AUTHORITATIVE.

FACTS

The National Survey reveals that the average audio tape of Elijah Muhmammd (30 minutes) will cost you approximately $8.00 or more!

Not only are our tapes of equal length as low as $6.95, BUT with a membership discount of 20% off, you only pay a low $5.56 - over 30% lower than anywhere in the country!!!

~ ~ ~

We send our tapes through a graphic equalizing and noise reduction process to eliminate unwanted hiss and noise. Why?

~ ~ ~

We're designed to do one thing - very well!

MEMPS MEMBERSHIP
Now Only
$30.00 per year!

You will save over $20 to $30 alone on just one purchase! The same $20 or so you would have spent elsewhere. Invest that extra cost in a membership and never worry about high prices again!

Please put me on your membership list for _____ MEMPS membership.
I have enclosed $ _____ and you may mail it to:

Name _____

Address _____

City _____

State _____ Zip _____ Phone _____

Only $30 per year

Send payment to:
MEMPS P.O. Box 162412 • Atlanta, GA 30321

WHY NOW IS A GOOD TIME TO BECOME A MEMEBER?

* First Automated Fax Retrieval of Elijah Muhammad Documents
* First Comprehensive Concordance
* First Comprehensive Subject Index
* First Alphabetized Anthology of Elijah Muhammad
* Many Specialized Research Compilations
* Lots, lots more . . . .

These Powerful Research Projects Will Be Offered To The Public For The First Time!

Now Is The Time To Become A Member Before Membership Fees Increase!

Other Great Book Titles By

Elijah Muhammad

Messenger of Allah

★ The True History of Elijah Muhammad
- *Autobiographically Authoritative* (HardB.) $21.95
★ Message To The Blackman In America $ 9.95
★ How To Eat To Live - Book 1 $ 7.95
★ How To Eat To Live - Book 2 $ 8.95
★ Our Saviour Has Arrived $ 9.95
★ The Fall of America $ 9.95
★ Supreme Wisdom Vol. 1 $ 5.95
★ Supreme Wisdom Vol. 2 $ 6.95
★ Flag of Islam $ 4.95
★ Holy Qur'an (HB) M.M. Ali Trans. $21.95
★ The Mother Plane $ 6.95
★ The True History of
   Master Fard Muhammad (HardB.) $16.95
★ Christianity versus Islam $7.95
★ The Secrets of Freemasonry $6.95
★ 100 Answers To The Most
   Uncommon 100 Questions $ 6.95
★ History of The Nation of Islam $ 6.95
★ The History of Jesus' Birth & Death $ 6.95
★ The Science of Time $ 7.95
★ Blood Bath: The True Teachings of
   Malcolm X $ 6.95
★ Police Brutality $ 3.95
★ Jesus: Only A Prophet $ 4.95
★ Elijah Muhammad Meets The Press $ 4.95
★ The Tricknology of The Enemy $ 3.95
★ I Am The Last Messenger of Allah $ 3.95

WHOLESALE YES

COD's YES

ALL MAJOR CREDIT CARDS YES!

Shipping & Handling Not Included $4.00 1st Book & $.50c Each Item Thereafter

ALSO WORLD'S LARGEST COLLECTION OF AUDIO & VIDEO TAPES OF ELIJAH MUHAMMAD AVAILABLE IN OUR FREE CATALOG! (770) 907-2212

Membership ($30 year) will get you a 20% DISCOUNT OFF all books, tapes & photos plus a FREE SUBSCRIPTION ($12 yr. otherwise) to MESSAGE TO THE BLACKMAN MAGAZINE

MESSENGER ELIJAH MUHAMMAD PROPAGATION SOCIETY (M.E.M.P.S.)

CUSTOMER SERVICE: P.O. BOX 162412 • ATLANTA, GA 30321
BUS (404) 684-1277 • FAX (404) 684-1278